THE RUNNING
MIRACLE

—⁓—

THE RUNNING MIRACLE

THE STORY OF A YOUNG MAN'S DETERMINATION
TO OVERCOME A CRIPPLING CHILDHOOD INJURY

—⚏—

LAMONT J. THOMAS

WITH

ASHLEY M. GRAHAM

W

WARD STREET PRESS · SEATTLE

The Running Miracle
ISBN: 978-0-9844969-3-8

BOOK & COVER DESIGN BY VEE SAWYER

Dedication

I'd like to dedicate this story to my family and extended family of Shoreline/ Richmond Beach, Bhima Ruggiero, the Pigotti Family, the Slonecker Family, and Royages Easton and the Easton family. Keep striving for greatness.

Contents

HERE'S WHAT HAPPENED   1

THE HOSPITAL   4

RECOVERY   7

MOVING TO LYNNWOOD   9

THE HILL   12

BACK TO SEATTLE   14

PAIN   17

NEW SCHOOL   19

MY BIGGEST FEAR COMES TRUE   21

KICKBALL   24

FIRE DRILL   28

BACK PAIN   32

RETURNING HOME   36

GRADUATION FROM ELEMENTARY SCHOOL   43

SUMMER BREAK   45

SPORTS   47

MIDDLE SCHOOL   51

THE WALKER   54

BASKETBALL TRYOUTS   56

BULLIES   59

THE MARTIN LUTHER KING JR. WALK   62

THE ROLLER SKATING PARTY   65

BIRTH OF A POSITIVE MINDSET 69

THE NEIGHBORHOOD 72

MY GREATEST INSPIRATION 75

RUNNING TO EASE MY BACK PAIN 77

MY RIGHT SHOE 80

HIP SURGERY 83

WORKING AT GIBRALTAR 85

GABE 88

SENIOR YEAR AND THE DRAMATIC CHANGE 90

THE BONE AND JOINT CLINIC 92

RETURNING TO HIGH SCHOOL 95

MOVING TO SHORELINE 98

RUNNING TO RICHMOND BEACH 101

BEING PROFILED 104

DAILY REPETITION 106

NPR RADIO 109

TIGER MOUNTAIN 112

SHORELINE TO EDMONDS FERRY TERMINAL 115

WHAT I'VE LEARNED 117

THE RUNNING
MIRACLE

Here's What Happened

I was only two years old when my life changed forever. On March 28, 1990, we just pulled up to my grandparents' house in northeast Seattle. My grandmother unstrapped me and my younger brother, Jerome, from our car seats. My grandmother took Jerome into the house. She was away for only a moment. Chris, my older brother, and I got out of the car, and as I've been told, I was following Chris, and I must have wandered into the arterial street near our house. I was out of the car for just a few seconds, and BAM! I didn't see the car coming. I was hit and launched into the air. My body rolled several times along the concrete before coming to a stop. I was lying lifeless in the road.

Some of my neighbors witnessed the horrific scene and ran to my rescue. Luckily, one of them was a doctor who was able to perform C.P.R. (cardiopulmonary resuscitation) until medics arrived. The medics arrived and I was transported by helicopter to Harborview Medical Center. This was not the closest hospital to our house, but it is the level four trauma center in the city of Seattle, and with my apparent injuries I needed doctors who had experience handling this level of trauma. On arriving at Harborview, my family learned the extent of my injuries:

- Shattered skull
- Fractured jaw
- Broken arms
- Broken legs
- Broken neck
- Shattered pelvis

Other injuries included brain trauma that caused seizures, migraines, dramatic mood swings, temporary loss of speaking functions, and nightmares for years to come.

I never did meet the driver of the car that hit me or learn very much about her, other than she was seventy years old and was visually impaired in one eye. I can't imagine the emotions and the suffering she must have felt after hitting a toddler.

I am not angry at the person who hit me; it was not her fault. Instead, if I had the chance to meet her I would say, "thank you."

To most, being hit by a car and suffering severe injuries sounds like a tragedy, but for me this tragedy turned out to be one of the greatest gifts I'd ever receive. The battle ahead would be a terrific journey. I am grateful that I can share the gift that grew from this tragedy.

The Hospital

—⚋⚋—

I spent three weeks in the trauma center at Harborview. After I was stabilized, I was transferred to Children's Hospital, where I stayed for about four months to begin my recovery and rehabilitation. I was always a happy kid, and in being so young, I was unaware of the extent of my injuries. I know now that the head injury I suffered was the most severe of my injuries. It affected my right side. Luckily for me, this is not my dominant side. Because of my head and neck injuries, I suffered partial paralysis on the right side. I was unable to move my arm and leg at all for most of my stay at Children's Hospital.

I was placed in a wheelchair/stroller device that also included a plastic vest and a halo around my head to prevent further damage to my neck and jaw. My jaw was shattered and wired shut. I stayed in the wheelchair and halo apparatus for ten weeks, essentially in the same position all that time. The one thing that I was able to do during this period of recovery, and loved to do, was paint. In fact, it was good therapy for my broken arms and sprained wrists.

Throughout my recovery, the doctors did the best they could to help me. Gaining strength in my body was the most difficult thing for me because of my severe head injury. Not only was I not able to move my right side well but my right side did not grow at the same rate as my left side.

The back injury I suffered caused an unusual curve in my spine, which made it difficult to sit up straight without severe pain. According to the doctors, I would never walk again or never surpass the brain mentality of a seven-year-old child. It was assumed that I would be bound to a wheelchair the rest of my life. Whether it was my age, or the severity of the brain injury I suffered, I was completely unaware of my condition and my surroundings. In fact, between the ages of two and five, I have very few memories due to the swelling in my brain.

Despite all of these injuries, I kept a smile on my face and continued to defy the long odds that were stacked against me.

Recovery

—⁓—

I was released from Children's Hospital, but I was not out of the halo, the plastic vest, and wheelchair apparatus I had been in for months. If that wasn't bad enough, I also had a tube running through a hole in my chest into my lungs to assist with my breathing. The tube was necessary to ensure that my lungs would not collapse until I could breathe on my own again. With all the tubes and craziness surrounding me, I still smiled in every picture taken of me.

While recovering at home, I grew stronger over time. It didn't happen right away, in fact it took a few years, but eventually, I did what the doctors said I would never be able to do again: I was able to walk. Of course, I had to support myself using a walker or crutches, but hey, I was walking and out of that wheelchair.

During my recovery period, I was able to attend preschool in the Queen Anne neighborhood of Seattle. Although I was disadvantaged because of my injuries, when the time came, I did not miss any school. I was able to start kindergarten at Olympic View elementary school in the Northgate neighborhood of Seattle, staying on track in school for my age.

Moving to Lynnwood

W hile I was in the hospital, my family had moved to Lynnwood, Washington, a suburb of Seattle. As I grew older and progressed in my recovery, I also moved further away from the Seattle hospitals and the support they provided. In a way, I went from having medical staff always available to help at the hospital to a big house with five siblings who also needed varying levels of attention themselves. It was a big transition for me. Because I had sustained my injuries at such a young age, I did not know how to do "normal" kid things. I didn't know how to ride a bike. I had rarely played outside. Everything was a new experience for me as I grew stronger and gained the strength to do fun, kid activities.

I loved race cars and race tracks. I went crazy over anything to do with Hot Wheels. You can imagine my excitement when my parents bought me a Hot Wheels race car bed. This was the first bed I would ever have that wasn't a hospital bed, at least that I can remember.

I was so excited! I wanted to jump into my new bed. But a simple kid activity like jumping into bed was impossible. My body wouldn't allow me to do it. Actually, half of my body could do it but the other half needed a push. With a little practice I was able to at least get in and out of my new bed on my own. Jumping would have to wait.

In third grade, I attended elementary school in Lynnwood for the first time. Most of the kids that went to the school lived around me, but I didn't know most of them since I was fairly new to the neighborhood. At school I was quiet and just tried to fit in, but when I got home it was a whole different story. I have two older sisters, Cassandra and Deangela, an older brother, Chris, and two younger brothers, Jerome and Kunga. Unlike at school, back at home I felt like I could be part of the playtime activities that kids do, without being self-conscious of my disabilities.

The Hill

—〰—

For years I watched my brothers, Chris and Jerome, ride their big wheels down the big hill by our house. It was a steep hill and they went fast! It was thrilling to watch them pick up speed down the hill and stop on a dime just before they would have catapulted into the lake.

I wanted to be able to do what all the other kids were doing; I wanted to feel the rush of going down that hill. I was determined to make that happen. One day, I followed right behind them up this big hill using my walker, with my big-wheel tricycle in tow. I had to sit on the concrete to get onto the trike, and it was not easy to get balanced properly. Once I was ready, I pushed off with my good leg and down I went! The first few times I did slow test runs, riding just half-way down the hill. It was going well. At the half-way point, I could drag my foot and turn quickly into the grass, which helped me come to a stop.

After a dozen successful tries, I was ready to go all the way. My first full run was a great success, so there I went again. Unfortunately, the second run was not so seamless. Down I went, picking up speed, faster and faster, but then my front wheel started spinning around and I couldn't control the trike. I couldn't slow down!

I cried out for help, but before anyone could respond I was in the lake, and my prized big wheel was in the lake next to me. The front tire had a hole in it and was ruined. In spite of my broken bike, it was a victory and it was fun. The adrenaline rush was awesome. It felt great to be just like the other kids, even if I was the only one who ended up in the lake.

Back to Seattle

—〰—

After years of my comfortable life in Lynnwood, we moved back to Seattle to move in with my grandparents, which was the same neighborhood where the accident occurred. I was in the third grade and not excited about switching schools. Also, I was not too keen on the idea of sharing a small house with so many other people, especially after living in our big house in Lynnwood. My grandparents' house had only two bedrooms, and there were all of us kids in the house. I had to sleep in the hallway outside of the two bedrooms.

As kids, we made the best of the situation. One of my favorite games to play in the house was called "King of the Mountain." This was a two-storey house, and the flight of stairs that separated the floors became our prime playing space. Since we slept in the hallway, we could line up our mattresses in a row down the stairs. The "king" would stand at the top and stop anyone from passing at all costs. Anything was fair game, except using my walker to stop intruders. The king could push, shove, kick, or punch. It was all part of the game. We suffered some injuries throughout the course of these games, but we were lucky that we never broke the window at the bottom of the stairs. When King of the Mountain got boring, we would get rid of all but one of the mattresses and fly down the stairs on our stomachs, crashing into the walls on the way down.

As much as I loved playing those games, what I really loved was being outside. Anyone who knew me knew that. Every day I would take my walker and go. I was like the neighborhood security guard; if there was something suspicious, I would point it out and tell someone. Many of my neighbors started calling me the "king of the neighborhood." Patrolling several blocks, I would walk back and forth all day. These long walks kept me smiling. Later on, I also did odd jobs for neighborhood folks, like mowing lawns or washing cars. I liked being active, despite the pain in my back and in my legs.

Pain

—✠—

For me, pain was a constant irritation. During this time, my spine vertebrae were rubbing against each other, and I couldn't stand up straight. The kids at school often called me the "black hunchback." I would wake up several times every night from back and leg pain. It felt like I was being stabbed constantly. It didn't matter whether I was walking, sitting, or laying down; there was no relief from the pain. On top of this, I was angry about the pain because it seemed to me like nothing was being done about it.

The doctors kept advising me to get more physical therapy, but I had been getting physical therapy and my condition had not changed. Later, I learned that because of structural problems with my back, the physical therapy was not helping. In fact, it was making the pain worse.

New School

—✺—

It was the first day at my new school in Seattle. While most kids are worried about making friends, I didn't have time for that. I was worried about more fundamental problems. How was I going to get down the hallway to class with my four-wheeled walker without drawing attention to myself? Of course, that is not possible. But once I finally made it to class, I relaxed a little bit and was excited to meet all the new kids.

The day slithered along. I was getting restless. I asked my teacher when I would go to my next class and where it was. "Oh Lamont, you will be in here with me all day." I was not used to sitting so long. I started to feel claustrophobic; my legs started to cramp. I couldn't wait until lunch. I watched

the clock as it ticked along slowly, min-
ute-by-minute.

Lunch was my favorite time of day. I was
finally out of the classroom, and I had regular friends at lunch that I knew from Special
Ed class. Some of the Special Ed kids were
in for violent behavior, and having these
boys as friends worked out great for me. I
knew that counting these boys as my friends
helped to deter others in the school from
bullying the new kid with the walker.

My Biggest Fear
Comes True

—◊—

On the very first day of school, after lunch, the day took a turn for the worse. I was sitting at my desk, unsuspecting. From across the room I heard a voice call my name.

"Lamont Thomas?"

I thought I was in trouble. Little did I know that being in trouble would have been better than what was about to happen. I raised my hand half-way, understandably apprehensive.

"It's time for your physical therapy," the voice said.

My stomach hit the floor. Physical therapy in itself doesn't sound so bad, but I was already dealing with kids laughing and pointing at me and my walker. I just wanted to fit in, and no other kids were going to physical therapy. It was yet another reminder that I was different. I reluctantly went with the therapist. I'm sure she could sense my frustration. I felt like she tried to embarrass me in from of my entire class!

The therapist made me do my stretches. I did them as quickly as I could to get out of there. Though seeing the physical therapist never helped my pain, I continued to see her three days a week despite my aversion to it.

The second time I saw the therapist, I asked her nicely to not announce my name and physical therapy in my classroom when she came to get me in the future. This seemed like a reasonable request, and she agreed.

However, on day three she did the same thing. "Lamont Thomas, time for your physical therapy."

I was so mad. And embarrassed. She did it AGAIN! So I ignored her just as she ignored what I asked. After saying my name a few times, she left the room. It was a victory! Well, kind of. I eventually gave in and went with her, but after that day she treated me differently. I stood up for myself, and I think she finally saw that treating me with some respect was really important to me.

Kickball

〰️

I was not shy when it came to asking to play something or do something. I didn't consider myself different; I just saw a walker in front of me, and with it, and it's four wheels, I could do anything.

Usually during recess, I would run around the field, talk to my friends, and shoot hoops. But this day, just beyond our group in the other corner of the playground, I saw some kids playing kickball. I resisted asking to play, fearing their reaction. Judging by previous comments from this group of kids, their response to my request probably wasn't going to be nice.

I longed for the opportunity to play with them. Thinking about it longer, I wasn't going to let them stop me because of what they thought. If I was tough enough to play "King of the Mountain" with my brothers and sisters, then I could play kickball.

My heart was racing as I walked up to them with my chest out and my head held high. "Hey guys. Can I play?" I asked.

Laughing at me they said, "How are you going to play? You can't even walk straight."

I couldn't say anything. I was humiliated. I hung my head and walked away. I just wanted to disappear at that moment. I was mad, sad, and hurt all at the same time. I started to question for the first time what was wrong with me. Why won't they let me play with them?

I felt sorry for myself, but not for very long. Instead, I decided that I was going to prove all of them wrong. My "I'll show you" attitude took over. From that day forward, I did not care about the pain. I wasn't going to let it stop me from what I wanted to do. And more importantly, my new goal was to show all those kids who teased me and told me I couldn't do something that I could do it. I had to prove to myself that I could do anything I wanted. I'd show them.

Over the next several weeks, I focused on trying to play kickball. Sometimes I would practice with my brothers and sisters, mostly pitching so I could watch how they did it. When it was my turn, I used my four-wheeled walker and put all my weight on the handles, freeing my legs to kick the ball as hard as I could. I also practiced running the bases with my walker.

After improving my kickball skills and building confidence, I once again asked if I could play. This time I was less nervous. In my head I though, "they said the wrong thing to the wrong kid." I was going to show them. All those kids who were mean to me, I was going to make them pay. Besides, their words were very hurtful and they deserved it.

"Go ahead, let him try. He'll probably just strike out anyway," a little girl's voice said.

As I approached the plate I was so nervous you could probably see me shaking.

What had I gotten myself into? Can I really do this? Well, here goes nothing.

"Strike one!"

My emotions go the best of me. I told myself to pull it together. Prove them wrong. I heard the pitcher talking trash about me. I blocked that out, focused on the ball rolling toward me, and kicked as hard as I could.

WHOP!

The ball went flying into the outfield. I grabbed my walker and ran toward first base. The look on their faces was priceless. From that day forward, I became more confident and realized that my walker didn't make me weak, just a little different.

Fire Drill

—∿—

I never experienced a fire alarm in person, but what I knew about them I did not like. The thought of being in a second floor classroom and having to get out of the building quickly stressed me out. Fire alarms depressed me because they confirmed to me and everyone around me that I was physically disabled. I hated that. But also, because of my disabilities, I was in danger. So, you can imagine my fear when I was sitting in class and I heard that loud, "BZZZZZZZZ" sound, knowing it was the fire alarm!

"Everyone quickly hurry out to the field and line up by your homeroom number," my teacher shouted. I rushed as quickly as I could, but with my walker, it was a struggle to get out the door quickly. I rushed down the second floor hallway toward the stairs with no plan of how to get down them. The noise from the alarm was loud and disorienting. A group of teachers realized my predicament and asked me if I could walk down the stairs.

"Maybe," I replied. What I really wanted to do was throw the walker down the stairs and descend the stairs from a sitting position. But that was a liability and not allowed, which meant I was slow to move and needed help.

"Well just come on and try," one teacher encouraged. Accepting that as my only option, I slowly made my way down the stairs, looking back the entire time watching for a raging fire to come racing my way. Now I was at the bottom of the stairs. Three teachers and I were the only ones left in the building; all the other kids made it out of the building much quicker. I was so embarrassed.

But, I made it! I found my homeroom number 203, and there I was in line. Alive! I survived the fire! About five minutes later I hear over the loud speaker, "Okay kids head back in to class and take your seats quietly." What? Go back in? I thought there was a fire? I was confused.

Turns out there was no fire, just a drill. Could have fooled me as adrenaline filled by body while scrambling with my walker toward the door. Knowing ahead of time that it was just a drill would have been nice, but hey, how else are you going to be prepared. Lucky for me I was on the first floor when that drill happened next.

Of course, I did not make it through the rest of the year unscathed. Every day for weeks I sat in my second floor classroom and watched the clock, anticipating the "BZZZZZZZ" of the alarm.

To my dismay, one day it happened! It was 1:45 P.M. and all through the school the alarm bell filled the halls. It was so loud, like a fire-truck siren right next to me. However, I had learned an alarm does not necessarily mean there is a fire. In fact, most likely it's just practice. Since then, I was able to relax a little more during future drills by telling myself there was no fire.

Back Pain

When I was ten years old, I had surgery to have my tendons stretched. Over the years, my tendons had become too tight for me to stretch on my own.

After the surgery, I was in a spica cast, which is a body cast that locks the hips and thighs in place so that the tendons could heal. I was in this cast for about eight weeks.

As I grew older and stronger, I started to be more active; I was able to do the outside activities I loved. But this proved to be more than my body could handle. A few years after my tendon surgery, I started to have horrible back pain. The pain on my right side was so intense I could barely move. I couldn't sleep; I would sit up all night crying from the pain. As unbearable as it was, I had no choice but to push through it and continue on with my life. Eventually my mom took me to the doctor to find out what was wrong. The doctor said I needed to have surgery to place poles in my legs to try to straighten the direction of my feet. Correcting the defects in my gait caused by the paralysis on my right side would help fix the curve in my back from scoliosis (the sideways curvature of my spine) caused by the car accident.

I was too young to understand exactly what surgery really entailed or any of the risks. But what I did know is that the doctor said I might be able to walk straight and pain free. That was all I needed to hear. For the next few days I imagined myself in a pain free body. All the things I could do. The longing for a body without pain took over. I couldn't wait to get the surgery.

The day before the surgery, I said goodbye to my teachers and classmates. I didn't know when I would see them again. I hoped it would be soon that they would see me running around without my walker and out of pain, doing everything they do. We got to the hospital early that next morning to check in. The doctor discussed the risks of the surgery in detail. Though I was only twelve years old, I was able to understand that really bad things could happen if there were any complications during the surgery. At this point I was more scared than excited. I wanted to back out, but at that age that was not my decision.

I was wheeled into the operating room where they placed an IV in my arm and just like that, I was out. The next thing I knew, I was in a hospital room with another spica body cast covering my entire body from my shoulders down. I thought to myself, "This is going to be okay."

Maybe it was the medication talking, or maybe it was just early enough in the recovery. The five days I spent in the hospital were not too bad. A lot of people came to visit; I had a TV and I had food, and every time I felt any pain I could hit a button that would give me more pain medication. By day four, I began to grow tired of the hospital. The next day, I was released to go home. I was a bit nervous about the move back home while still in my cast, but I thought the change of scenery would be good.

Returning Home

Oh boy was I wrong! I had no idea how good I had it at the hospital. The first test came just trying to get me home. At first it was funny. My step-dad had a hatch-back Honda. He tried to fit me in the front seat sideways. It wasn't working with my body cast. Luckily, after about thirty minutes of struggling, an ambulance offered to take me home. Returning home proved to be challenging. I was embarrassed that I relied on everyone for everything. I mean everything! My body hurt from being in one position for long periods of time in the cast. Being stuck in that cast got old quickly. And at twelve years old, it was hard to understand why everyone else could do what they wanted, but I was stuck in a dumb cast.

My neighbors would come by and visit periodically, which cheered me up a lot. On one particularly awesome day, my neighbor, Don, stopped by. As he walked toward me, I saw a two-feet tall trophy in his hands. It was a bowling trophy, but he took the ball off the figure at the top so that it looked like a man running.

Cool, I thought. But as he got closer I saw the inscription on the trophy. It read:

Lamont Thomas,
King of the Neighborhood

I was ecstatic! This trophy meant so much to me. I couldn't stop staring at it for at least a week. I came from a family of athletes, but given my condition I could not play sports competitively, so the thought of getting a trophy never crossed my mind.

The thrill of the trophy lasted for a while, but eventually I became quite sad and lonely. My family carried on with their lives. They would leave me at home and go out to dinner and the movies. They usually brought me back something, which was nice, but at twelve years old, I thought it was unfair that I was stuck in bed and they weren't.

The healing became more and more uncomfortable as the incisions from surgery began to heal and itch. I was warned by the doctors about the potential risk of infection if I do scratch at it so I tried not to. Although, after discovering that a hanger would reach down my leg, I refrained from using it too much fearing it would erase all the healing that happened and set back my recovery. After a few months the itching subsided, but life was still pretty boring; watching TV and movies is only entertaining for so long I learned. And I was going crazy because I hadn't been outside in months, my favorite place. Things were slowly getting better though.

This was all happening right in the middle of the school year. I was currently a fourth grader and had about five months of school to cover to graduate to fifth grade. So my teacher started coming to my house to homeschool me. I liked my teacher so I had no problem with this. During the second week of her visits, she surprised me and brought the kids from my class to visit. The kids brought a gigantic banner that they all signed and it read, "well wishes" and "get well soon." They even brought me a hand held basketball game to play.

Over the coming weeks I learned to occupy my time writing. I could process my thoughts quicker that way since I was still struggling with my speech. This was a creative outlet for me. I would write song lyrics, poems, you name it, I was writing it. Writing helped me develop a much better vocabulary, and it also lifted my spirits, which I really needed at that time.

By the eighth week, I never wanted anything more than to get out of that cast! And finally the day arrived. I heard the words come out of the doctor's mouth, "you're healing up great. It may be time to get you out of that cast." I started crying. I was so excited at the thought of moving my legs and the ability to go places again.

I was excited until I got to the doctor's office. In an instant, my joy was tainted by fear as the saw required to cut through the cast was in view. I asked, "What you are going to do with that?"

The doctor replied, "We're going to cut the cast so don't move."

I was scared he was going to cut me or even worse — saw my legs off. My imagination went wild with the possibilities. The doctor cut three ways, once up my leg, once down the stomach. My heart was racing. Finally, the last cut was completed and I was free! The doctor said, "Try to walk."

Acting like it was nothing; I took a step and instantly my legs gave out. I fell to the floor. I was laughing uncontrollably. The doctor said, "Don't do anything too crazy. Your legs haven't been moved in a while and atrophy has set in."

This was not good because my right leg was already atrophied before the surgery and the cast. But like all things in my past, I was confident and ready for it. I wanted to walk unassisted and straight. This was my opportunity, but things didn't happen quite that easily. After the cast was removed I experienced the worst itching and indescribable, excruciating pain that I would experience in my life so far. I had Charlie horses, shooting pain, and horrible itching every day. I wasn't in much better shape than I was with the cast on. Now the pain was preventing me from doing the things I wanted to do. I could get to the itch now, but I was scared to scratch it for fear of causing an infection and having to start all over again.

A few weeks after getting the cast off, a physical therapist came to my house to help me start strengthening my body again. At first I was not cooperative with her. I didn't get the point of all the exercises. I was in pain and her exercises were part of the problem!

She said, "It's going to hurt at first but as you grow stronger the pain will subside."

I didn't believe her. But she was right. The longer the physical therapy went on and the more I did the exercises, they got easier and the pain subsided some. I started to be happy with the changes I saw in my body. I started to test myself by walking one block at a time. I did this for eight weeks because graduation from elementary school was in eight weeks. I was so excited. My plan was to be able to walk across the stage for my fifth grade graduation and get my diploma without any assistance. I probably could have done this, but unfortunately my teachers wouldn't let me because they were scared I would fall. I was so mad. I worked so hard, but I wasn't going to give up and stop there.

Graduation from Elementary School

The day was finally here — graduation! I was excited but a little nervous. My legs were only a few months out of the cast. With all the atrophy that happened over that time, it was a little tough to move around freely. Not to mention, my walker took up the space of three people. We had one rehearsal the day before. We all lined up as though it was the real thing. I was placed on the right corner. Standing for two hours during the rehearsal was almost more than I could bear, luckily I had my walker to sit on. However, this walker was the source of a lot of argument. I wanted to take the picture without my walker. My teachers would not allow it, but I kept pushing. I didn't win. I now understand it would have been a liability for them to let me walk across the stage with no walker. I could have been hurt.

So here it was the next day. The day of graduation. I was filled with emotion, nervousness, excitement, anxiety; I was everything but angry. I was not a big fan of getting up in front of people, but I wanted my diploma. They called my name and I made my way across the stage, walker in hand. I could see everyone's eyes following me each step I took. I had no choice but to look in their direction. Finally it was over. I made it across without falling or tripping, or anything more embarrassing than the walker. I could finally relax. I left that school the same way I came in — smiling!

Summer Break

—〰—

Over summer break, my siblings and I set up a lemonade stand. One of us, most often it was me, would stand on the corner holding the sign yelling, "lemonade 25 cents!" We made $400 over that summer selling lemonade. I don't know if it was all the sign holding and screaming or if it was because I knew everyone in the neighborhood. Most of the people gave us more than asking price for the cup of lemonade. One person even gave us $20! It was a great way to start the summer and something we'd continue for summers to come.

To make for an even better summer, I knew I had a birthday party coming up. My birthday was July 29th and my brother Kunga and sister Deangela had their birthdays in August, so my parents decided they would throw us a combined birthday party. It was the best party ever! There was a bouncy house in the yard, a clown, which I was terrified of, and other fun activities. I tried out the bouncy house, but my balance failed me. I could barely stand up, and the kids kept falling on me. After a few minutes I got out. I was able to have fun, hang out with friends, and participate in all the other activities. It was an epic birthday.

Sports

My family loved sports. I have three brothers and two sisters. All of them played sports. My older brother, Chris, and my two younger brothers, Jerome and Kunga, played basketball, football, and baseball. Deangela played baseball. I spent lots of time watching them play.

It was hard for me to play sports with the walker, but I didn't let it stop me. With my brothers, we would all go in the alley and play basketball, either horse, 21, 2-on-2, or around the world. My eldest brother Chris was very talented. At a young age, he was six feet tall. He had mad dunking skills too. Anytime he'd get on the court, it was going to be a good game. My younger brother Jerome was a hooper too, very competitive.

Let's not forget my youngest brother, Kunga. He's got skills too. He could maneuver in ways I've only seen on TV. We all had the basketball gene, only I wasn't as fortunate due to the car accident. But that never stopped me from trying.

All of us were playing in the ally behind our house. The neighbor had a fenced yard but their basketball hoop hung over the fence, so that's where we played day after day. A lot of trash was talked on that court. As I grew stronger I would go there often to think and shoot around. I constantly tried to improve so that I could play without everyone being concerned that I'd get hurt.

I knew I probably would fall on our basketball court, but I had to try. I put aside the walker, and shot all by myself for about a half hour. I wasn't very good, but the fact that I was able to be out there was enough for me. I got along with my brothers well, and even though they were ten times better than me, I was just happy to be part of the team. Occasionally my cousins would come and play with us. I enjoyed just watching and laughing at all the trash talking. One day we were all playing all the games we knew. Out of nowhere, my brother Chris dunked so hard the entire hoop came down with him! Instantly everyone ran! My brothers took off! I trailed behind using all of the speed I had. I finally made it back to the house laughing uncontrollably.

My sisters both played softball for a few seasons when they were younger. Meanwhile, my brothers all played for the local football organization, Shoreline Univac. I would often go to their games but be very discouraged and sad that I couldn't play. It made me depressed and angry that I was unable to play. Being overshadowed by a family of great athletes was tough. They were all allowed to play sports, but I wasn't because I was handicapped, disabled, or whatever you want to call it. It made me ask why? My mother told me she was afraid I might trip and fall. All kids trip and fall, I thought. Why am I being singled out? Years later I found out that one bad fall could result in injuries serious enough to cause paralysis. It was a risk my mother was not willing to take.

One of the hardest parts about sports was that I understood what they were telling me about my limitations, but I refused to accept it. I knew I was different simply by the way people stared, but I did not consider myself disabled. My thoughts and mindset were never focused on my disabilities. I was happy with who I was. I just felt really upset when I was treated differently. My family is such a positive influence on my life, development, and character. I looked up to them, and as I reflect on my purpose in life at this moment, that feeling is still strong. Times were very stressful, but we got through it together.

Middle School

—∿—

After graduating elementary school, and with my fun summer coming to an end, it was time to prepare for middle school. I was assigned to go to McClure Middle School in Queen Anne. I was excited about middle school, but nervous because everyone I knew was going to a different school. I wouldn't know anyone at my new school.

Despite this, I felt prepared for the challenge. I got up for the first day of school really early. I heard the screeching brakes of the bus outside. I ran out and hopped on. On our way to school we picked up nine other kids. We got to school about twenty minutes early, which gave me a chance to scope out where my classes were ahead of time. To my dismay, my classes were not close together. My second class was at the other end of the school. With my basic (non-wheeled) walker and my legs not being strong enough, I was never going to make it on time. I was worried. Luckily the teacher was aware of my situation and allowed me to leave class early to get to second period on time.

It was fine that I could get to class on time, but I hated the sound and the attention the walker would attract. "Clink, clink, clink," down the hallway I went. I got so fed up I thought that using the four-wheeled walker would get me to and from quicker, plus I could always sit on the back of it if I got tired.

I signed up for swim classes to continue strengthening my legs. I was excited about that, but I had to make it across the street to the pool. I had a ten-minute head start, but I would still be late sometimes. The swim teacher was understanding and lenient with me.

I knew how to swim; I was actually pretty good. I had been doing it for my physical therapy the majority of my life. I always felt comfortable in the water until one day something happened that I was not prepared for. Many of the boys would horseplay in the water. I knew better than to participate. But one day it was not my choice. I became the victim of horseplay.

I got into an argument in the deep end of the pool with this new kid, who wasn't really one of my friends. I tried to end the argument and swim away, but he wouldn't let that happen. He sat on my shoulders and pushed me under water. I am not sure if it was his intention to try to drown me, but he held me underwater so long I felt like I was starting to lose consciousness. I used all the strength I had and lifted him off of me.

After I got out of the pool I wanted to chase after him and punch him. But I knew I didn't have the strength in me after all of that. I had to let it go. Weeks later, we talked it over and dealt with it. But this was a pivotal point in my life. I knew somehow, some way, I had to get stronger.

The Walker

—〰—

I started refusing to bring my walker to school because I felt it was a crutch. I would never get to where I wanted to be if I continued to use it. I needed to build up the strength in my legs, and the walker was halting that. However, this was a bit of a safety hazard. Mentally, I was strong enough, but my legs weren't quite ready. I was only a year out of my full-body cast. I had to give in and keep using the walker for a while.

So instead, I started to walk a lot further and instead of using the walker to support my weight I started to push the walker along so I could become less reliant on it.

When I would get home from school I would ditch the walker and walk three to four blocks without it to test myself both physically and mentally. Even when I knew my legs couldn't make it, somehow I would. I just kept pushing through the pain. It was during one of these trips I experienced an anger-driven endorphin high. This was dangerous because I was pushing over boundaries that I was advised not to do, but I didn't care. I wanted results. By the blessing of god, my attitude paid off. I could feel the strength building; I was in lots of pain, but that in itself added to the adrenaline rush.

Usually when pain hits, you're supposed to stop. But I was in pain all the time, so I really couldn't tell the difference between overdoing it and normal pain. This led me to think I could do just about anything!

Basketball Tryouts

—⚏—

One day, I saw a poster advertising that the school was having tryouts for the basketball team. And in the spirit of being able to do anything, I decided I was strong enough to play. I was going to try out. Finally, I would fit in with my sports-centered family. Maybe I wouldn't feel so left out if I could get on the team. People who doubted that I could do things like play basketball because of the way I looked upset me so much. I would do anything to prove them wrong.

At this point, I was using the walker only at school. I wasn't using it at home because I was strong enough to walk without it for quite a distance. People's assumptions about me were based on things other people said, like the doctors, other kids at school, people who didn't really know me and understand who I was. I had more mental fight in me than anyone else I knew.

When I saw that poster for basketball tryouts, there was no way I was going to miss it. I desperately wanted to be on a team and win some games. My thoughts were racing with all the excitement that would come from playing competitive sports.

When I got to the tryouts the coach said, "Everyone must get a waiver from your doctor to play and you must maintain a 2.0 grade average to be eligible to play in games."

I said to myself, "I got this in the bag."

After school I scheduled an appointment with my doctor. He said, "You aren't quite strong enough, and I don't feel like it would be safe for you to play."

I was so disappointed. But, I didn't let this keep me down for too long. I turned my sadness into adrenaline. I was going to show my doctor that I was strong enough. I met with the coach. He was very understanding and sympathetic to my situation. He decided that I could be a manager for the team. I would travel with the team and manage the clock at home games. Most of the kids were nice to me and made me feel like a part of the team. I contributed my positive attitude.

Bullies

—m—

Things were going well. I was on the basketball team, sort of. The kids were being nice to me for the most part. However, there were a few kids that were not so nice.

This one time, I was already having a difficult day. On my way down the hallway, walker in hand, I ran into these kids. These bullies thought it would be funny to take my walker and throw it down the stairs. This was the fourth time I had been bullied since starting middle school. I said to myself, "I am not going to take this anymore."

The teachers and principal did little to stop any of it. So I stopped using my walker or any support for walking. I needed to be able to defend myself and the walker was just asking for trouble. I figured without the walker I would no longer be a target. Oh was I wrong. The kids called me names like cripple legs, and even retarded. They were just making fun of what they saw.

None of them took the time to find out why I walked the way I did. But I went on with my day as if that was the norm, ignoring their insults. I wanted desperately to get rid of my walker for good. The teachers threated to call my parents if I stopped using the walker. I didn't care though.

Eventually I gave in, figuring that the only way I'd reach my goal of no walker was to do the exercises and work with the physical therapist. As much as I hated being called out in class for physical therapy, it was something I tried to embrace, finally.

I still had the physical therapist that came to my house too. I was not only hesitant at school but also at home. I was embarrassed to do my exercises at home because there was always someone around watching me. After a few months I got over this hesitation and embarrassment. I was determined, and I wouldn't let any distraction stop me from obtaining my goal.

The Martin Luther King Jr. Walk

—⌇—

For the Martin Luther King Jr. holiday, my school sponsored an essay contest. I submitted an essay to the competition, and mine was chosen as one of the winning essays. I was excited that my essay was selected. Not only was I excited about the prize, but I was thrilled that I could write something that was award worthy.

A few weeks later we had an assembly where the winners of the essay contest were announced and the prizes were handed out. At this assembly, they also announced that we would be participating in a walk. We were to walk from the school to the Seattle Center.

The Seattle Center was exciting. It had rides, the Space Needle, and a fountain to run in. But for me, there was a big problem. My school was at the top of Queen Anne hill and Seattle Center was at the bottom of the hill. The Queen Anne neighborhood has several of the steepest streets in all of Seattle. How was I going to make it down the hill with a four-wheeled walker?

We started off on our walk; after four blocks, we started down the first small hill. "This is going to be easy," I said to myself. Little did I know what was coming. As we continued a few more steps there it was: the biggest, steepest hill I had ever seen in the thirteen years of my life. All the kids continued like it was nothing, but for me one slip could have me rolling all the way down the hill with nothing to stop me but a car or the concrete. I was terrified, but I made it down after about forty-five minutes. A teacher stayed behind and helped me.

On our way down, I noticed we were being taped by a KOMO 4 News camera.

I wondered what story they were covering? When I saw myself walking on the TV, I realized I did not look right. All this time I thought I walked fairly straight. Boy was I wrong. My foot was completely inverted, but correcting it hurt my right leg and it would make the leg really tired.

After seeing how I walked on the news, I didn't care anymore. I told myself I would no longer take it easy anymore. I would push boundaries, doing everything I could to walk better. I set my goal. By the end of middle school, I would walk without my walker, and I would be stronger than I have ever been. From that day on, I started walking a block more every day until I was satisfied with my progress.

The Roller Skating Party

—◊◊◊—

J ust before the end of seventh grade, there was a roller skating party that every seventh grader would attend. It was our reward for all the fundraising we did throughout the year. I raised a lot of money over the year, but I knew I wouldn't be able to participate in roller skating with my lack of balance. In fact, due to the liability, my parents and the school wouldn't allow me to participate. Though I can look back and understand the reasons, I was so angry. My anger and sadness consumed me. It was unfair to me. I busted my butt to make this happen, and I couldn't be part of it.

In lieu of skating, my parents gave me twenty dollars to play video games at the arcade, but that soon dwindled to nothing, and I was upset that I couldn't skate. I hated sitting around. It depressed me to see the other kids having fun while I sat there and watched.

At that point it had seemed my whole life had been that way — the multiple surgeries, the unfixable back pain. I finally just said I'm done feeling this way, I'm done having a walker, I'm just done! Something got into me that next day, and I felt it the moment I woke up. Everything I did revolved around me being "disabled," but I refused to let myself be defined this way.

The next day I came to school with a new, confident look on my face. As I walked down the halls, some of the kids asked, "Where's your walker."

"At my house," I told them. The kids looked at me like I was crazy, limping down the halls.

When I passed the teacher in the hallway, he asked me the same question. Where was my walker? To which I replied, "I don't need it. I can walk without it!"

I was tired of everyone asking me this question, as if I was committing a crime. When my teacher asked me if I got permission from my doctor, which of course I hadn't, he made me follow him to the nurse's office to get a walker to use for the day. I was furious. The look on my face on the way there told it all.

The nurse asked me again, "Where is your walker? Why don't you have it with you?"

I lost my cool. I couldn't take it anymore. "Look I don't want to use it anymore. I am the target of bullying, and am being harassed, and you have done absolutely nothing about it."

The nurse replied, "Well, not using your walker is a hazard and a liability." Then she followed with a statement I didn't quite understand at the time. "You may be suspended or kept from going to school and we will have to contact your parents."

To which I replied, "Go ahead, I'll dial the number for you."

Ultimately, I won the battle. They gave up. It was the perfect time for me; before this I had been so sheltered by all the people around me. Finally, I had the opportunity to stand up for myself, and this time it actually made a difference. It was a very empowering moment for me. I felt that if I could function without my walker, I should have the opportunity to do so. At this point, I didn't care what the doctors thought. Telling me that I had to use the walker was saying I couldn't do something or be anything more than disabled. It made me angry.

Birth of a Positive Mindset

—⁀ஸ⁀—

After winning my fight with the walker at school, I started to see things differently. I was in control of my destiny. Not the doctors who said I wouldn't walk on my own; not the kids who laughed at me when I wanted to play sports; not my teachers who doubted me; not even my family who treated me like I always needed help. I learned that what others had to say had little bearing on my life, and I took control. If I continued to live the life others saw for me, I would never excel.

I started walking countless blocks trying to gain strength in my legs, doing what the doctors said I'd never be able to do. I made it forty blocks from my house one day, and the pain began to mount. It became almost unbearable, but I had to make it back home somehow.

I tried to not get discouraged and upset, as this would not help me. I turned up my music and began pushing forward with my strong leg while the other leg struggled to keep up. The further I got, more adrenaline rushed through my body. I kept track of my time so I had something to beat each day. I was in competition with myself. I was going to do whatever I had to do not to be "that kid with the walker."

As I got closer to home, the adrenaline wasn't enough. The pain was bad, but I had to keep going if I was not going to be that kid anymore. I had to push through the pain to build the strength.

As my tailbone was digging into my lower back, or so it felt, I just kept going. The spasms might have slowed me down a bit, but they didn't stop me either. Every day I fought to go longer and faster. The neighbors liked seeing me walk by every day, and I loved seeing them. They were all so supportive.

The Neighborhood

As I got older I learned more and more about my accident. Some of the neighbors still lived in the area and would tell me more about it. I learned that it not only affected me, but it also affected many of the people who witnessed the accident and who knew my family. Learning more about it made me feel very connected to the community and the people in the neighborhood.

When I still had my four-wheeled walker, I would ride it like a chair yelling, "Lamont's in the house!"

The walker was loud enough on its own, but it felt good to announce myself and be noticed. I scooted around the neighborhood at all hours of the day. I bet I kept the rate of home break-ins down since I was always around watching what was happening.

Since I knew all the neighbors well, I started to put my entrepreneurial skills to good use. I started to earn money any way I could. I washed cars, did yard work, baby sat, anything I could. It wasn't always easy. Sometimes half way through a yard work job my leg would give out. But I had to finish if I wanted to be paid. So I always pushed through until the end. Luckily, there wasn't much competition in the neighborhood. No other kids were out doing what I was doing. I started with the four blocks around my house then expanded further into the neighborhood asking my neighbors every weekend if they had work I could do.

I worked all year, rain or shine. There were times when the work I was doing made me cross the very street where my life was almost taken from me. It got me thinking a lot about the accident. I sort of knew what happened to me. But what about the lady that hit me? What happened to her? How far did she drive before she realized she hit me? All I knew were stories I was told by other people, people who lived on the street and heard about it. I guess after my accident the city put a speed limit sign in that spot. They reduced the speed to 35 MPH. Before my accident this street was more like a highway. It comforted me to know that it was no longer as dangerous.

My Greatest Inspiration

—〰—

Some of us are lucky enough to have someone to keep us in line growing up. For me that person was my grandfather. He was the enforcer in my life. Just one look from him said it all, and I'd know if I was in trouble. He almost never raised his voice; he didn't have to. He taught me so much about life. His words were few and far between, but when he did speak, it was profound.

He was the hardest working person I knew. He is my model for drive and endurance. He worked as a security officer at a building downtown. My grandpa woke up early all week long. So he liked to sleep in on the weekends. I woke up early from the pain. It often didn't allow me to sleep. One morning I tried to take a shower early. The bathroom was close to his room and it was impossible for me to not make a bunch of noise. I woke him up that morning and the look he gave me could have killed. Needless to say I never did that again.

Though we were all scared of him, he played a role in our lives most people wouldn't have taken on. There were six of us, and he helped us all grow into the people we are today. I am who I am today because of his strength, persistence, and incredible work ethic. He passed away from cancer just before my high school graduation. I took comfort knowing he was looking down watching me as I crossed the stage. He knew that I could overcome the odds the doctors placed on me. He is still with me today, and he is a big reason why I aspire to be a role model to kids all over.

Running to Ease
My Back Pain

—⟋ᴍᴍ⟍—

After all the surgeries I had gone through, I suppose I was happy I could still walk at this point. However, I was upset that no one seemed to listen to me when I told them about the pain I was experiencing. I guess because they had no idea why I was having the pain or how to treat it.

I went to physical therapy and a chiropractor. With little success I was sent back to the specialist. They tried injecting me in the back with steroids, which I had to have every six months. The steroid shots hurt like no other pain I experienced. As soon as the needle was inserted, every nerve in my body was on fire. Inserting the needle happened very slowly, and was far worse than any benefit from the shot.

I was getting tired of waiting for someone to fix my problem. I had arthritis in my hip and lower back as well as scoliosis and severe back spasms. The surgeons already told me there was no surgery to help, and it would likely only make it worse. I was tired of being at everyone's mercy. So I did the only thing I knew to how do, run through the pain. Running and music were the only escape I had.

For me, I first started running at age fourteen. Actually, at first it was more like speed walking. My walker had wheels so I could hold the bars, shift my weight to my hands, and start to move my legs as fast as I could. The adrenaline rush was intoxicating. I started thinking that maybe someday I could run on my own. At first it was one block, then two blocks. And so on. I could run forever, as along as the battery on my Walkman didn't die. Back then we didn't have fancy cell phones to listen to our music. People would ask me, "doesn't running make it worse?" Maybe it did, but the music pumped me up and the endorphins released from the running helped to override the pain. I was happy to have found some relief from the pain. Even if it was very temporary. Even if it was only helping while I was running, it was a few minutes I spent not in excruciating pain.

About six months later, I was able to speed walk/run without the walker. Again, I had to start slow. At first it was one block, then two blocks. I would play Michael Jackson on my Walkman and headphones and just go. My back really hurt, but I pushed through. After this point, whenever I was physically capable, all I wanted to do was run.

My Right Shoe

I was constantly having issues with my right foot. It would drag. I didn't have the ability to point it straight due to the weakness on my right side. This resulted in many of my shoes being destroyed on the right foot in the right corner. If I played any sport or even just walked, within two weeks I would need a new shoe. Meanwhile, my left shoe was like new.

This was a big issue for me. You see, I was part of the Air Jordan era. Everyone I knew would have a new pair of Jordan's. My brother, Chris, had them because he played a lot of basketball. And he got more new pairs than me. It seemed very unfair. I only got a new pair every once in a while. There was no point in paying for some really expensive shoes when my right one would need to be replaced in two or three weeks at the most. My parents probably spend $200 a month on new shoes for me, and that was for low end shoes.

To try to straighten my leg, the doctor prescribed an ankle-foot orthosis, or AFOs for short. These were specially made casts for your feet. My initial understanding was I would slip them on and then place my shoes on over them. The only problem was that I wasn't able to fit them with any of my new shoes, so I had to go buy ugly cheap shoes. And by ugly I mean ugly. The shoes with the big Velcro straps, like old people wore.

I was very picky about these shoes. I had to find ones that didn't look horrible, if that was possible. I wore the AFOs for six months. With them on, I wasn't able to turn my ankle or walk inverted if I tried. They were comfortable, don't get me wrong, but the real issue was with all the restriction they caused. I couldn't really do anything I wanted, like play sports, because it restricted me from walking like I normally would. We saved money on shoes, but to me it wasn't worth being slowed down. And I still couldn't wear the shoes I wanted.

When I took them off, I was surprised at how much straighter I was able to walk. Before the AFOs, I would have to think about pointing my feet the right way. After the AFOs, it just happened by itself. It didn't take away the pain I had in my leg though.

Hip Surgery

—ᴍ—

At age sixteen, I had another surgery, this time for my hip. Over the years, the difference in my gait along with the partial paralysis on my right side caused damage to the hip. I swayed left to right, but due to the weakness on my right side, my right hip took a beating. I was in so much pain. Often, I would just try to deal with it by walking or ignoring it, but eventually I couldn't take it anymore.

The hip surgery was needed to correct the damage. After the surgery, I was in another spica cast for about eight weeks, just like the cast I needed for my tendon surgery. I spent a few months healing, and I began to feel so much better. Also, my back was no longer sinking and I could stand up straight much longer, rather than needing to slouch. I was so much happier due to the absence of pain. I started speed walking again, and then I began to run, challenging myself to see how fast and how far I could go. I could do things others told me I could never do. I played more basketball, and got pretty good at it, and I played football, as the quarterback. I had two good years after the surgery, but then, the pain returned, and I needed another operation.

At this point, your probably wondering how in the world my family could afford all of these major surgeries. Well, they couldn't. My medical care over many years, which included multiple surgeries and countless out-patient treatments, would not have been possible without assistance from the Washington state Medicare-Medicaid program. Every time I required more medical attention, the Medicare-Medicaid program was there to help me get the care I needed.

Working at Gibraltar

———

That summer I had been playing basketball at a local park. My friends and I played literally every day. I loved it! I didn't have many outlets. Running and writing were the only others. Writing helped me process my thoughts. I could write song verses as well as poetry.

One day while at the court, I met a person by the name of Bhima. Me and my buddy loved competition so anyone that came on the court we wanted to play. This day we were just shooting around, and I had mentioned my interest in learning about real estate. Bhima said that he worked at a local real estate office called Gibraltar. It was only five minutes from the court. He said he would see if I could possibly get some volunteer work hours there to learn about the business. I was excited. I had never been in an actual office, at least not to work.

The opportunity was a huge blessing. I arrived at the office and began with mailers. I had to learn a lot. I didn't even know how to fold the paper. I was doing all this while finishing high school. It was a lot to take on, but I loved the time I spent there. I never imagined that it would turn into something more. A few months into my volunteering, I was offered a job. I was hired part-time to mail fliers mostly. Over the first year, Bhima taught me a lot about advertising. After learning all this, I began to work in different departments. The skills I learned over the first year I applied not only to my job but also to my life. My first day and many to follow I showed up to work in my beloved jerseys and jeans. I soon realized this was not proper work attire. I was not aware of any dress code at the office, and at the time I was not a fan of dressing up. Who wants to be uncomfortable all day? However, I switched it up and took note of the others around me. Luckily those around me showed me the way.

In the coming weeks I stopped wearing jerseys and finally saw how nice it felt to be noticed for something other than my limp or the fact I couldn't walk straight. My first suit was an all-black pin stripe suit with a vest. I loved wearing it, but soon it became a new thing for me even outside of the office. Outside of work, I wanted to represent Gibraltar and myself in good fashion, and it didn't hurt to see the shock in the eyes of people when I walked down the street dressed professionally, not in a jersey. I retained that job, and I am still there, currently in my eleventh year. I was blessed with this opportunity and couldn't be more humbled.

Gabe

—⁓—

There are people who just by being themselves bring out the best in you. They help you capture a moment of happiness when you feel really stressed. At Gibraltar, my friend Gabe did that for me every morning, sometimes just by telling a joke, or doing an impersonation and goofing off. It was powerful because he was always simply himself, purely genuine. He would go out of his way to help anyone, regardless of what he had to do. I looked forward to coming to the office because I never knew what the day was going to bring.

I was friends with Gabe for several years, and one day, he was driving on the freeway and was in a head-on collision. He passed away from his injuries. It was a difficult thing for me to understand. But I was able to pull strength from what Gabe showed the world. What he gave the world was a picture of kindness. He showed me that one act of kindness can travel distances and affect others. He was the type of person who wanted to make you laugh, engage with you, and make you smile every time he saw you. Because of Gabe, I try to apply these principles to my life every day to make a positive impact on others. I want to make sure his legacy lives on. Though he may not be with us physically, he is present spiritually, in me.

Senior Year and the Dramatic Change

—⚬—

I was looking forward to going into senior year. I had a pretty easy senior year ahead of me, having satisfied the majority of my credits already. I was really excited to have reached this point with all the tough work behind me.

Though the school work was behind me, all the pain was not. I heard the same thing from my doctors over and over again. "It's normal. You'll be fine." That didn't satisfy me and didn't help with the immediate pain I was in. Since the doctors weren't much help I sought the help of my therapist. I walked into his office crying one day from all the pain. Clearly he could see something was wrong. I had been seeing him for years, and he had never seen me in such bad shape.

The pain I kept feeling radiated up and down my body. I just ignored it, as I was used to doing. And with good music playing in my headphones my mind could be taken away from almost anything. I kept running and pushing through the pain for months, but eventually it became unbearable. Since my doctor seemed to just write off my pain with no good explanation, I asked if I could see a specialist. After months of complaining, she finally sent me to see someone who could help.

I was so frustrated with the doctor for not listening to me and letting me live in excruciating pain for so long that I learned a lesson from all of this. I wasn't a very aggressive person, and sometimes I would just let things go. However, this experience taught me that sometimes I needed to be a little more outspoken and stand up for myself. It wasn't often that I got as mad as I was at that doctor.

The Bone and Joint Clinic

—❦—

Finally, I got an appointment to see the specialist, someone who could finally help me. From the specialist, I found out the majority of my right hip joint was gone. My hips were so uneven from having to use one side predominantly that the cartilage had worn down and the bones were grinding on each other. I needed to have yet another surgery, a second surgery on my hip, a hip resurfacing surgery, where they would replace my hip socket but leave as much of the original hip bone as possible. They set a date for February, which was right in the middle of my senior-year classes. Luckily, the school was very understanding, and I was still going to be able to graduate despite the time off school I would have to take.

Entering the surgery, my biggest concern was how long it would be until I could walk again. No one could give me a definite answer. As always, the doctor went over all the risks of surgery. It scared me, but I was determined to be able to run and walk without excruciating pain. And at this point, the pain was so bad it was starting to affect my outlook on the future. Running was my outlet, a way to relieve all my stress, and with all the pain I was feeling I couldn't even do that anymore. I decided the risks were worth the potential benefit.

I thought after the surgery I would once again be confined to some type of cast restricting my walking. From all my previous experiences, I was definitely not looking forward to this. But I was wrong, they actually had me walking right away. In fact, they insisted I walk on the new hip socket right away. For the first time in a long time, I was able to walk with little pain. It was mostly just muscle weakness from the surgery that I had to deal with.

With the absence of pain I was very motivated to get walking and keep walking. The doctors said it would take six months to a year to fully recover. I laughed and said, half joking, "I only need three weeks." I wasn't sure how long it would take, but I knew I hated the crutches they gave to me. It was almost worse than lying in bed because with the imbalance in my body, all the work was coming from one side, and I would get severe pain and massive bruising on the right side from the crutches slipping around. This was all the motivation I needed, and in exactly three weeks I was able to kick the crutches.

Returning to High School

By the time I returned to school from surgery, I had missed a good part of senior year. It was already February. The teachers decided I could be excused from the senior project. But I wanted to do the senor project.

I chose to do my project on a famous poet. It definitely challenged me. There were a lot of words I did not know, and with my memory loss it was hard to remember all the words and their definitions. As difficult as it was, I knew with repetition I could retain all I was learning. I would study for days and days, but as soon as my mind was taken elsewhere it was as though I forgot all I was learning on my project. I was so frustrated and worried that I wouldn't pass and graduate. For the remainder of the school year my focus was on that project. I was working twenty hours a week at Gibraltar, so the rest of my time was spent working on the project.

Part of the project was a twenty-minute presentation. This was probably the part that worried me the most. I had terrible stage fright. There was no way out of giving the presentation, and as the day got closer I became more and more scared. When the day finally came, I was literally shaking. I couldn't chicken out. I approached the stage and took the mic. I took a deep breath and tried to keep my voice from shaking. I started speaking, and in all, it went pretty well. I was able to remember all that I needed to. I only messed up a few times.

Although the presentation was over, the stress wasn't. I still didn't know if I passed and would graduate. Luckily, this stress only lasted a few days. I soon learned that I got a B on my presentation. I was elated! A huge feeling of relief came over my entire body. I sat and thought about all my life how many times I thought I couldn't do something. And at this moment, I felt prouder than at any moment in my life. Adding to my excitement, I found out I was one of two kids from the district receiving an award for all-around excellence from The Breakfast Club, which was a club that acknowledged over-achievers. I was nominated by students and teachers for the award.

About a week later I received another award from the Rotary Club of Seattle. This one included a $2500 scholarship for college. I was overcome with emotion when I heard about this award. As hard as it was to get through high school with all the pain I endured and all the time taken away for surgeries and doctor's appointments, my efforts did not go unnoticed. Now I could focus on planning my next step in my school career.

Moving to Shoreline

---~~~---

Moving forward, I attended Shoreline Community College in Shoreline, Washington, a suburb of Seattle. I wasn't sure what I wanted to do yet but I wanted to get started with college. I took three classes while I worked. I took law, business, and math.

Again, I struggled with remembering the things I was learning. It wasn't a good start, and it made me nervous about my college career. But just as I made it through high school and my senior project, I was determined to make college work for me as well. My law class was my favorite. I was intrigued with all the information, and I diligently listened and took notes. Unfortunately, it was not enough. I got extra help, but still failed the class. Just having someone recite information to me was not the way I learned. I felt discouraged, but I learned later on that I had to teach myself in ways that would help me retain the information. I am a very hands-on learner, and typically the teaching styles in my college classes didn't emphasize that method.

Though discouraged, I wasn't going to give up. That wasn't my style. I signed up for the law class the next quarter, hoping that repeating the class would help me retain the information. Taking the class a second time did not help. It had me more confused. I got so upset and angry with the situation. In addition, because of my brain injury, performing well on tests was very difficult for me. With these limitations, it was difficult to succeed in college.

In the meantime, I had been running, which helped me relieve my anger and frustration. I would run for blocks and blocks until they became miles. I was determined to defeat the statistics and prove the doctors wrong about the healing time and what I would be able to do. Though I would feel pain when running, I knew that if my body resisted, my mind could overcome it and I could achieve it. Once I had my mind set on something, I did it.

Running to Richmond Beach

—◆—

Richmond Beach was one of my favorite places, a beautiful beach and park right on Puget Sound. It was 2.3 miles from my family's house. I had been there many times by car and bus. I was still recovering from surgery and in quite a bit of pain, so I continued to go there by bus. But after about three bus rides, I decided I was going to walk all the way there.

I knew it would be hard as I was still struggling with my right side being partially paralyzed. There was a big hill to get down and a ton of stairs to get down to the beach. But I didn't care. I knew if I set my mind to it, I could get there. I loved the endorphin rush that came from exercising. As I started to walk, those endorphins took over and the pain and exhaustion in my body disappeared. After about half-way down the stairs to the beach, the pain in my spine started shooting. It was so frustrating that I used it as my motivation to keep going. I kept pushing through. On my way down I spoke to people about my condition. It took me numerous attempts before I reached the beach. I finally made it! However, my pain was so severe that I was forced to catch the bus back home.

I was a fighter, and fighting with pain was a big part of it. It pushed me beyond my boundaries. A lot of people didn't understand what I was doing or why I would put myself through all the pain. Some of these people made assumptions about me and started to spread rumors about me, like I was a crazy person, or that I was in a skateboarding accident. Despite all of the negativity around me, I continued to walk daily. It was a way for me to escape the negativity and all the doubting from my doctors. When people said I couldn't do something, that was my motivation.

It took me years to walk all the way to Richmond Beach and then back home, but I kept pushing through and finally made it. I walked that same route for seven years. I started to run a block or two, which eventually turned into a mile or two. My own competitiveness pushed me to keep running, to compete against my earlier self. I was motivated by good music and the sounds of people bullying me and telling me I couldn't do it. I wasn't a slow runner. I loved to race people on my route. I also loved to jump. I would jump up to touch signs or whatever was within my reach while I was running. I became known as that guy who jumps and touches crossing signs. I assumed at this point people knew who I was and knew my story.

Being Profiled

—∞—

I guess not everyone knew who I was. Running my regular route down to Richmond Beach, four years into my running adventures, I was pulled over by a cop.

He said, "Sir what are you doing?"

"Running, sir," I responded.

The officer replied, "I got a call a crazy black man was jogging up and down Aurora Avenue."

He asked for my ID, which I didn't carry when I ran. I mean really, who does? Coincidentally, across the street were two white men jogging. I respectfully asked the cop why he didn't stop them. Of course he had no good answer for that. I knew I had done nothing wrong and though I didn't pass law class, I started to remember a lot of it in this moment. After he looked up my name, he saw I was clean and let me go.

I walked off laughing and thinking, "So that's profiling, huh?" And of course I didn't let this detour me from running. Interestingly, a few months later I was in almost the same spot running when I saw flashing lights approach me from behind. This time someone called the police because they saw someone fall down several blocks from where I was who matched my description. The officer stopped me to ask questions about the incident.

I asked the officer, "If I was injured, wouldn't I still be in the place where I fell?" I guess he agreed after I stated the obvious, and I walked off. Luckily, I haven't been bothered since that day. Besides, focusing on negativity never gets you anywhere. I focused on the people in the community who were supportive. My purpose was to show them that with a positive mindset you can do anything you set your mind to. I wasn't going to let a little racial profiling stop me from that.

Daily Repetition

—⚭—

I kept on with my daily walks and runs. On the route many people would stop and ask me, "Why do you walk so much?" or "Why are you walking so far? Where are you going?"

I would tell them, "It's because I've been waiting seventeen years to walk with no assistance and finally I can. I walk because I know what a blessing it is to be able to walk."

A few months later I learned that a student at a local high school made a fan club for me on a social media site called, *The Random Guy Who Walks/Runs In Jerseys around Richmond Beach*. I was shocked. Partly because I wasn't exactly popular when I was in school and now a good majority of this school, and the neighborhood, knew who I was. Soon after, I was contacted by a local paper, asking if I would do an interview.

Of course, I agreed. I wanted to share my story with everyone. I wanted everyone to know why I walk. I wanted them to know how walking and running helped me overcome all the pain in my body. Mostly, I hoped my story could provide inspiration to others going through their own struggles. The interview went well.

Later that year I got just that chance. One of my good friends, Alex Meyer, called to tell me that a radio station wanted to interview me. Alex worked at KOMO News, and he had a connection with a DJ at KMPS radio who was interested in my story. I was ecstatic. It's not like these types of opportunities come very often. They interviewed me over the phone while I was in my office. I was nervous when the interview started, but my nerves settled as the interview went on. I was able to share my story with everyone listening to country station KMPS in Seattle. It felt great!

And I guess a lot of people heard or read my story because after that, as cars drove by, people would honk and yell. It took quite a while before I realized they were honking and yelling at me. Then someone ran up to me and said, "I heard you on the radio — you're famous!" It was a great feeling.

I didn't feel famous though. I was just a guy who lost the ability to walk three times, so I was on a mission to walk until I couldn't anymore. Something most people took for granted, I didn't. I wanted to inspire a change in the attitude of others by sharing my story of persistence. I didn't let my injuries and setbacks stop me and neither should they. If I could inspire one person, I could potentially inspire hundreds, even thousands.

NPR Radio

About a year later, I got the call I had been waiting for my whole life. Sharing my story with the local paper and the Seattle radio station was a great honor, but now my dream was finally going to come true. I was going to be able to reach so many more people. Apparently, a local parent who knew my story saw my Facebook fan page and passed it on to a national radio station.

I got a call from a writer at KUOW, the local NPR station. She heard my story and wanted to interview me. Prior to the interview, I did not know the impact the interview would have, or how far it would reach. I spent a lot of time thinking about what I wanted to say, and I felt ready for the interview.

The interview was supposed to take place while I was running but, the weather didn't cooperate — as it often doesn't in Seattle. There was thunder and lightning. I didn't mind. I ran in any weather, but the interview took place in a small SUV. As the interview started, I got very nervous and everything I practiced saying slipped out of my mind. I was so nervous! I had to improvise and answer the questions honestly. Some of the questions asked were, "Why do you run? How did you get started? What drives you to keep going?"

I answered with a simple response that I thought satisfied all the questions, "Because doctors told me I never would." This interview wouldn't be that simple though. She wanted a more in-depth answer. I thought for a few minutes and finally came up with an answer to her questions. I guess people liked it. A few weeks later I checked my fan page and the number of followers went way up. People were telling me they loved me and what an inspiration I was. I hadn't thought of myself in that way. I was just glad I could tell my story and others could take from it.

That NPR interview played another six times for the next several weeks. I continued to receive support on my Facebook fan page and in the community. It was unbelievable, and it motivated me to do more.

Tiger Mountain

―ᚨᚱᚢ―

I felt so inspired from all the people around me, I wanted to do more. I decided to push myself both physically and mentally. I was terrified of heights, so this was going to be one of my biggest challenges ever. My friend, Alex Meyer, was going to climb Tiger Mountain, in Issaquah, Washington. I decided I was going to do it with him.

We started off early one morning to the mountain. There was a mile and a half walk before we made it to the mountain's trail head. On our way to the mountain we saw paragliders going off the mountain way at the top, around 2500 feet above us. I looked up and asked Alex, "Is that where we're going."

"Yep!" He replied.

We started up the mountain. The trail was quite narrow in parts and we had to share the trail with people going down. It left very little room and got me very close to the edge of the trail and the mountain. My heart raced faster and faster as we ascended. I knew there was nothing keeping me from falling off the side of the mountain. I kept my head down focused on the trail and kept moving one foot in front of the other.

My back started to radiate pain up and down my body. My right leg was feeling more and more weak as we continued. I ignored the pain. It never stopped me before, and I refused to let it stop me on this day. As we reached nearer and nearer to the peak, my leg became more and more exhausted. We reached an outlook point and it was absolutely amazing.

Hopeful, I asked Alex, "Is this the top?"

He responded, "Nope, almost."

As we continued the climb, the path began to expand wider. The hills were not as steep, and there was really no room to fall off the cliff. A sigh of relief rushed throughout my entire body. When we reached the top, the fatigue, the pain, and happiness were all circling me as I conquered another goal.

My life has been complicated, amazing, and one of the greatest gifts one can receive. The love and respect of people in my community, those I allow to enter my life, and those yet to be placed in my path going forward, are placed there for a reason.

We made it down the mountain successfully, and I was exhausted. But when I got home I knew I had to set another goal for myself. I started planning my next journey. With the mountain, I conquered height. My next goal would be for distance. I had the mindset and drive to do just about anything. I just had to control the pain until I completed my goal.

Shoreline to Edmonds Ferry Terminal

—∿∿—

After thinking long and hard about my next fitness challenge, I decided one Saturday to get up and start walking. I had no destination. I had been to Edmonds, Washington twice. Both times I was in a car. I pondered how fast I could get there by simply walking. I looked on my GPS, and it showed that from my house it was 4.8 miles to Edmonds.

I stared the walk at 10:00 A.M. I thought a lot about how just eight years prior I had been attached to a walker, and now I am able to do things sometimes a normal working body cannot. I am able to push beyond what is medically safe for me.

I thought about how one doctor's simple comment, "you'll never walk again," sparked a fire in me that allowed me to take on everything I doubted I could do as a challenge I could conquer. I had an endorphin high the whole way. I knew my destination, and I would do whatever it took to get there as fast as I could. I walked as fast as I could up and down the treacherous hills. The pain shooting up and down my partially paralyzed leg acted as a reminder. But it just made me push even harder. I covered so much ground in a short amount of time. As I raced around the last corner there was a line of cars. People just staring. I started to laugh as I reached the beach and the Edmonds ferry dock. I laughed because I finally made it. I laughed at all the people who said I couldn't. I took another moment to reflect on just how much of a blessing this was.

What I've Learned

——∿——

Throughout my life I faced challenges and obstacles that I would never wish on anybody. It took me twenty-two years to feel like I succeeded in proving the doubters wrong. With every surgery to fix a debilitating medical problem, I faced setbacks. My life has been one of constant struggle. But I have learned not to give up. After reaching my current goal, I've told myself to keep pushing, to continue striving toward accomplishments I did not think I could achieve.

I'm not boasting. And I do not feel my struggles make be better or stronger than anyone. I strive to be better than myself each day. I acknowledge my differences and accept everyone else's because those differences are what make us unique. They are what make us, in a word, us. When we learn to acknowledge differences, we learn to accept them. If you believe in something, continue to do it no matter what anyone else tells you. If you want something, strive for it, every day.

What you dream, you can achieve. And you just might inspire others to do the same along the way.

More about Lamont J. Thomas

—∿—

Lamont J. Thomas would like to connect with his readers through any of the communication channels listed below. Feel free to reach out to him to ask questions or share your thoughts about his story. If your organization would like to invite Mr. Thomas to speak to a group of students or employees, please contact him by phone or email.

Cell Phone:
>   206-902-8729

Email:
>   Lamontthomasseattle@gmail.com

Facebook:
>   /lamont.thomas.5/

Facebook Fan Page:
>   /lamonttheshorelinerunningmanthomas/

Twitter
>   @lamonttherunner

For more information about this publication, go to:

www.wardstreetpress.com

colophon

—ᴍ—

This novel is set in JANSON TEXT, an old style font designed by the Hungarian punch cutter Miklós Kis in 1685. The modern day digital version is based on Hermann Zaph's work at Stemple Foundry, where he found the original matrices created by Miklós Kis. *The Running Miracle* will share this beautiful and enduring typeface.

WARD STREET PRESS
SEATTLE, WASHINGTON

WWW.WARDSTREETPRESS.COM

CPSIA information can be obtained
at www.ICGtesting.com
Printed in the USA
LVOW12s0317290617
539750LV00001B/129/P

9 780984 496938